C000213047

SHORT CIRCULAR WALKS IN THE DUKERIES
BY
JOHN N. MERRILL

Maps and photographs by John N. Merrill

a J.N.M. PUBLICATION

1985

a J.N.M. PUBLICATION

J.N.M. PUBLICATIONS,
WINSTER,
MATLOCK,
DERBYSHIRE,
DE4 2DQ

a J.N.M. PUBLICATION

© Copyright—text—John N. Merrill 1985

© Copyright—maps, photographs and routes—John N. Merrill 1985

First published—October 1985

ISBN 0 907496 29 6

J.N.M. Publications, Winster, Matlock, Derbyshire. DE4 2DQ

John Merrill.

ABOUT JOHN N. MERRILL

John combines the characteristics and strength of a mountain climber with the stamina, and athletic capabilities of a marathon runner. In this respect he is unique and has to his credit a whole string of remarkable long walks. He is without question the world's leading marathon walker.

Over the last ten years he has walked more than 55,000 miles and successfully completed ten walks of at least 1,000 miles or more.

His six walks in Britain are—

Hebridean Journey ....1,003 miles
Northern Isles Journey...913 miles
Irish Island Journey ....1,578 miles
Parkland Journey ....2,043 miles
Lands End to John O'Groats ....1,608 miles

and in 1978 he became the first person (permanent Guinness Book Of Records entry) to walk the entire coastline of Britain—6,824 miles in ten months.

In Europe he has walked across Austria (712 miles), hiked the Tour of Mont Blanc and GR20 in Corsica as training! In 1982 he walked across Europe—2,806 miles in 107 days—crossing seven countries, the Swiss and French Alps and the complete Pyrennean chain—the hardest and longest mountain walk in Europe.

In America he used the world's longest footpath—The Appalachian Trail (2,200 miles) as a training walk. The following year he walked from Mexico to Canada in record time—118 days for 2,700 miles.

During the summer of 1984, John set off from Virginia Beach on the Atlantic coast, and walked 4,226 miles without a rest day, across the width of America to San Francisco and the Pacific Ocean. This walk is unquestionably his greatest achievement, being, in modern history, the longest, hardest crossing of the USA in the shortest time—under six months (177 days). The direct distance is 2,800 miles.

Between major walks John is out training in his own area —the Peak District National Park. As well as walking in other areas of Britain and in Europe he has been trekking in the Himalayas four times. He lectures extensively and is author of more than sixty books.

CONTENTS

Footpath Sign — Roche Abbey Walk.

INTRODUCTION

The walks in this book cover an area of land lying in eastern Derbyshire, the southern tip of South Yorkshire and the western side of Nottinghamshire. It is not rugged country walking but an area that boasts an incredible variety of historical buildings, which, as the area's name implies, were built by various Dukes. I have broadened the accepted Dukeries area because I felt there were other places in keeping with the Ducal theme that are well worth exploring and walking in.

In the north you walk to see the monastic ruins of Roche Abbey, see the majestic ruins of Thorpe Salvin Hall, walk beside the peaceful Chesterfield Canal and pass the imposing Barlborough Hall. On the eastern side in one walk you can visit three of England's finest buildings—Bolsover Castle, Hardwick Hall and Sutton Scarsdale Hall. The central area, the heart of the Dukeries, takes you to the caves of Cresswell Crags, and the extensive woodland of Sherwood Forest around Welbeck, Warsop and Edwinstowe. Other walks take you into more attractive woodland near Scarcliffe, Wellow and Walesby, while others are historical pilgrimages, such as Rufford Abbey and the walk to Eakring and its links with William Mompesson. The southern end of the walk area includes two memorable walks, from Southwell to the River Trent and back, and one through further woodland around Newstead Abbey.

In many cases the footpaths are only slightly used, but, unless stressed in the text, the route line, stiles and footpath signs are all there indicating the walk. In summer a few paths become overgrown or the fields full of crops and it may be necessary to walk round the field edge to get to the next stile. All the walks are circular, from a car park and in some cases both long and short walks can be done. There is at least one inn on every walk!

I have been walking in the Dukeries for the last fifteen years and I have enjoyed exploring the places so rich in history and legend. I hope these walks take you into the area and help you to discover its fascinating secrets.

Happy walking!

John N. Merrill.

JOHN N. MERRILL
WINSTER, AUGUST 1985

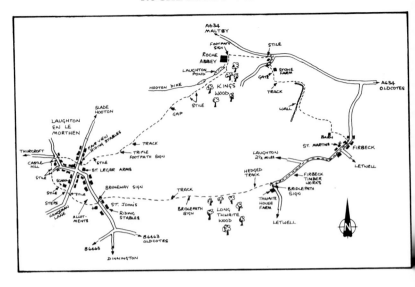

Roche Abbey.

ROCHE ABBEY—Cistercian abbey founded in 1147 and built from local stone. The buildings suffered extensively at the dissolution of the monasteries in 1538. A bonfire was made in the stalls to melt the lead off the roofs. The site, which is in a sheltered dale and particularly attractive in spring with the numerous daffodils, is now cared for by the Department of the Environment.

ROCHE ABBEY—7½ MILES—*allow 3½hours*

MAPS—O.S. 1:50,000 Sheet No 120—Mansfield and The Dukeries—O.S. 1:25,000 Sheet No SK 48/58—Kiveton Park

CAR PARK—No official one at St. John's or Laughton en le Morthen, where the walk starts. Car park at Roche Abbey.

ABOUT THE WALK—Starting from the road beside St. John's church you encircle the attractive village of Laughton en le Morthen, with its noble church spire dominating the area. Next you walk along the crest of the Slade Hills, which is magnificent walking, to gain the impressive monastic ruin, Roche Abbey.You return across fields on bridlepaths via Firbeck to St. John's. Whilst the walk starts from St. John's, being circular you can start it from Roche Abbey or Firbeck.

WALKING INSTRUCTIONS—Leave the road beside St. John's church, via the stile and South Yorkshire footpath sign. The path is well defined and is a track at first, before walking with a hedge on your right and allotments beyond. ¼ mile later reach Hangsman Lane. Cross over to your right to steps and footpath sign. Ascend the steps with a school on your right. Follow the path as it curves round northwards, with stiles to guide you and the church spire on your right. At the next road, turn right and 50 yards later on the lefthandside of the first bend, leave the road as footpath signposted and walk around the perimeter of the village, now heading eastwards. Less than a ¼ mile later reach the road from Slade Hooton. Cross over and follow the path beside Fair-View Riding School, signposted for Roche Abbey. 150 yards later on your right is the St. Leger Arms. Almost immediately afterwards at the end of the field, turn left and descend the field to a stile on your right, about 150 yards away.Here turn right and ascend gently to a track and triple South Yorkshire footpath sign. Turn left and follow this track along the crest of Slade Hills for a mile to King's Wood and a stile. Bear left and descend through the trees to a well defined path and turn right. Soon on your left is Laughton Pond and¼ mile later Roche Abbey.

With the tall ruins of Roche Abbey on your left, turn right, as footpath signposted and walk across the large open field, with a small stream well to your right. ½ mile later reach the A634 road. Turn right and right again almost immediately and descend the road to Roche Abbey Mill Farm. Ascend past the farm and turn left onto the lane to Stone Farm. Walk past the farm on your left onto a track. Just beyond turn left onto a grass track and follow this for¼ of a mile to a small wall on your right. Keep this wall on your right as you turn to your right; now heading southwards. ¼ mile later reach a track and turn left along it. A further ¼ mile the track turns right (southwards) and shortly afterwards left to road. Keep ahead on the track to a barn where you turn left and follow the curving track to Firbeck, reaching the road and bridlepath sign.

Turn right and walk through the village passing St. Martins church on your right. ½ a mile later the road divides; take the left branch, signposted Dinnington 2¾ miles. Pass the Firbeck timber works on your left and descend to the sharp lefthand bend in the road at Thwaite House. Leave the road here, at the bridlepath sign and walk up the track past Thwaite House Farm. Turn right past the house to gain a hedged track; now heading westwards. For the remainder of the walk back to St. John's 2 miles away, the track is well defined. First you walk past Long Thwaite Wood on your left before crossing the fields to St. John's. You reach the village beside a bridlepath sign. On your left is the church and where you started the walk.

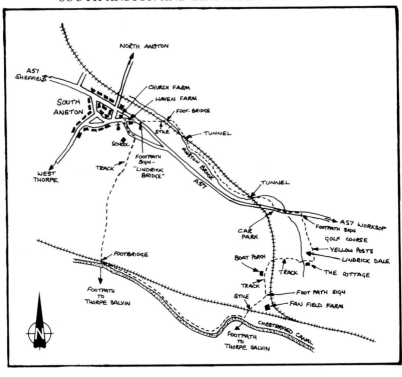

Footbridge and Chesterfield Canal.

SOUTH ANSTON AND LINDRICK DALE
—5 MILES—*allow 2½ hours*

MAPS—O.S. 1:50,000 Sheet No 120—Mansfield and The Dukeries O.S. 1:25,000 Sheet N0 SK48/58—Kiveton Park

CAR PARK—At Lindrick Bridge, beside the A57 road, at Grid Ref: 538828

ABOUT THE WALK—First you walk beside Lindrick Golf course before crossing the fields to the Chesterfield Canal. After 1½ miles beside it you ascend to South Anston before descending into woodland and walking beside Anston Brook back to the car park. A short but very enjoyable walk which can be extended by 3 miles to include Thorpe Salvin as detailed on the next page.

WALKING INSTRUCTIONS—From the car park walk along the A57 road towards Worksop for 250 yards and just past the road to Lindrick Dale, turn right as footpath signposted. The path follows the edge of the Golf Course, past the 8th Tee and is marked by yellow posts. Little over ¼ mile reach a hedged track and footpath sign. Turn right and at The Cottage 100 yards later left and follow the road which becomes a track shortly after turning right 50 yards later. Pass through the railway bridge and turn left, as footpath signposted along a track, passing a house on your right with an upright boat as a porch. Shortly afterwards turn right at the footpath sign and follow the defined path across the field to railway line. Cross this and reach the Chesterfield Canal.

Do not cross the bridge but turn right and walk beside the canal on your lefthand side for the next 1½ miles. At the third bridge—Thorpe Bridge—leave the canal and turn right and follow the path through the trees to the fields and defined path which you ascend to South Anston; much of the path is a bridleway and the last ¼ mile is a track with a school on your left. At the road turn left and 200 yards later on a sharp lefthand bend, with the church closby, turn right beside Church Farm. Follow the lane past Haven Station Farm to the A57 road.

Cross the road and follow the path signposted—Lindrick Bridge. First the path descends to the railway line and once over this the path soon turns right as you walk through woodland with the Anston Brook on your right. ½ a mile later walk though a railway tunnel and another ¾ mile later. On the other side the brook is now on your left as you ascend up a wide track to the A57 road and car park.

Boat Porch House.

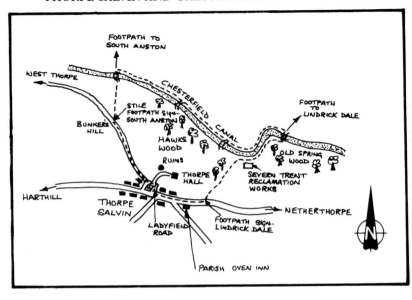

Ruins of Thorpe Salvin Hall.

THORPE SALVIN AND CHESTERFIELD
CANAL—3 MILES—*allow 1½ hours*

MAPS—O.S. 1:50,000 Sheet No 120—Mansfield and The Dukeries—O.S. 1:25,000 Sheet No SK 48/58—Kiveton Park

CAR PARK—No official car park

ABOUT THE WALK—You start at Thorpe Salvin an 'unspoilt' gem of the area, with a fascinating church and old font, and the ruins of a hall nearby. After a short road walk you descend the fields to the disused Chesterfield Canal, which you follow through woodland. You return over the fields to Thorpe Salvin. The walk starts just south of the church and can be extended to 8 miles by following the South Anston/Lindrick Dale walk from the canal. See previous walk.

WALKING INSTRUCTIONS—Turn right in front of the churchyard into Ladyfield Road. The road curves round to your left, with the churchyard on your left and ruined hall on your right. Keep on this road for ½ a mile to the top of Bunker's Hill where there is a stile and footpath sign on your right—'South Anston'. Turn right and descend the edge of the field with the hedge on your right. Just after entering the trees you cross Thorpe Bridge with the canal on your right.

Turn right and walk along the towpath with the canal on your immediate right for the next 1½ miles. At the third bridge, just after passing a series of small locks on your right, cross the bridge and turn right to follow the path through the trees of Old Spring Wood. At first you are not far from the canal but just over ¼ mile and guided by yellow arrows you move away from it to gain a track in front of a Severn Trent Reclamation works. Just afterwards turn left and follow the stiled path with Old Meadow Wood on your right. ¼ mile later reach the minor road beside the footpath sign—Lindrick Dale. Turn right passing the playing fields on your right before descending past the houses to Thorpe Salvin church.

THORPE SALVIN—The ruined hall was built by the Sanfords in the 16th century. Later it was owned by the Osbourne family and Sir Thomas Osbourne, who became the Duke of Leeds, lived here until 1697 before moving to a new mansion at Kiveton Park. Since then the hall has never been lived in and is now an impressive ruin. The church is particularly interesting with considerable Norman workmanship and an exceptionally fine Norman font.

CHESTERFIELD CANAL—James Brindley, who was born in Derbyshire near Wormhill and known as the 'father of British Canals', surveyed and planned the canal in 1769. It ran from Chesterfield to Worksop and Retford before joining the Trent at Stockwith. The canal was completed after Brindley's death in 1777. Today it is sadly neglected and the Derbyshire section was permanently closed following the collapse of the Norbriggs Tunnel—2,850 yards long—in 1908.

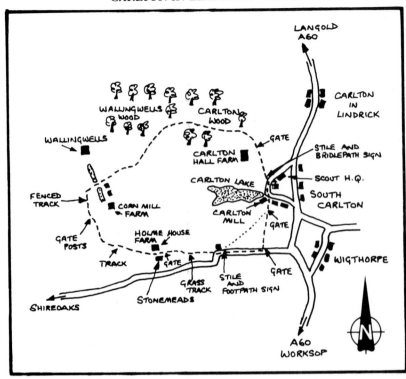

Carlton Mill.

CARLTON IN LINDRICK
—3 MILES—*allow 1½ hours*

MAPS—O.S. 1:50,OOO Sheet No 120—Mansfield and The Dukeries O.S. 1:25,000 Sheet No SK 48/58—Kiveton Park

CAR PARK—No official one, but parking room beside the church.

ABOUT THE WALK—A short walk around the Carlton area, through woodland and across fields, passing close to lakes and historical buildings. You enter Carlton beside its mill, and a visit to the parish church, dedicated to St. John the Evangelist, completes your tour.

WALKING INSTRUCTIONS—Start opposite the church with a stile and Bridleway sign. First cross a field to a gate with Carlton Hall Farm on your left. After the gate the path curves to your left close to the field boundary on your left, before entering Carlton Wood. Walk through the wood for just over ¼ mile, keeping straight ahead at all cross paths. Just after the fourth one you reach a corner of the wood, where you turn left and follow the well defined path across a field and on to two lakes. Walk between them, with buildings on your left, and ¼ mile away on your right is Wallingwells. Just beyond the lake reach a track and turn left and walk along a fenced path. After passing through a small wood and past large gateposts, gain the track to Corn Mill Farm on your left. Continue ahead to a Y junction and turn left along the track to Holme House Farm.

Pass the farm on your left, and at the righthand bend, with Stonemead House on your right, keep straight ahead to a gate and grass track. Follow the track and keep on it to the road ¼ mile away. There is a right of way to your left but it does not exist in the ground. There is another with stile and signpost just after reaching the road on your left, but in summer the field is full of crops and the pathline hard to follow. It is better to walk along the road for ¼ mile to the next right of way—a bridlepath—gained by the gate on your left. Cross this to the outskirts of South Carlton, where a stiled path leads you through the houses to the road and Carlton Mill on your left. Walk up the road to the church and walk starting point.

CARLTON—IN—LINDRICK—The church dedicated to St. John the Evangelist, is one of the oldest in Nottinghamshire, with Saxon window and masonry in the tower. Inside, the font is Norman and nearby are two garland brackets. Garlands can be seen in several churches in Derbyshire including Ashford in the Water. When a betrothed girl died before her wedding, a garland of paper flowers in the shape of a birdcage was made. It was carried in front of her coffin at the funeral procession and afterwards hung above the deceased person's pew. The custom was popular in the Midlands during the 18th century. Carlton Mill dates from the 18th century and the mill wheel can be clearly seen. It is now a museum.

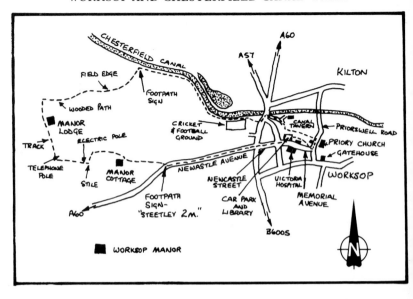

Manor Lodge.

WORKSOP AND CHESTERFIELD CANAL
—4 MILES—*allow 2 hours*

MAPS—O.S. 1:50,000 Sheet No 120—Mansfield and The Dukeries—O.S. 1:25,000 Sheet No SK47/57—Worksop (South) & Staveley

CAR PARKS—Beside Library on Memorial Road, where walk begins—Off Central Avenue, beside Chesterfield Canal

ABOUT THE WALK—Worksop, known as the gateway to the Dukeries, is full of interesting and historical features. Prominent is Worksop Priory which is passed at the start of the walk. Surprisingly you hardly see the busy shopping area before walking along the banks of the peaceful canal. You loop round the area to see the Elizabethan Manor Lodge, associated with Worksop Manor, which played a major part in both local and national history with the imprisonment of the captive Mary Queen of Scots here in 1570. A walk across the fields returns you to Worksop.

WALKING INSTRUCTIONS—Walk west out of the car park and into the gardens surrounding the Library and Museum. Walk through the grounds to Memorial Avenue close to the road junction with Priorswell Road, in front of Worksop Priory. Turn left and left again into Priorswell Road. Just past the lido and after crossing the river, turn left into the grounds and walk through them, noticing the car park on your left.Don't cross the bridge but keep ahead to Beaver Place, with the gas works on your right. Turn left into Church Walk with the Fisherman's Arms on your left. Continue along the road to Bridge Place. Just before it on your right is Canal Road, with the canal and Canal Tavern. This is as far as the Chesterfield Canal is navigable. Turn left at Bridge Place and right almost immediately into the car park. At the far end on your right gain access to the canal and turn left.

You now walk on the lefthand side of the canal for the next mile.At the wooden footpath sign turn left past a bridge and cross the new bypass. The path is defined and keeps to the righthand edge of the field. After½mile you cross a track and enter a wooden section with the remains of a canal on your right and the River Ryton on your left. Less than¼mile later reach a track and turn left and walk past Manor Lodge. After the Lodge Farm on your right you pass a small wood on your left before passing fields. Continue ahead for about 150 yards and just after a telephone pole turn left and cross the field, passing an electric pole at the other side. The path line here is faint but at the hedge is a stile. Over this turn left to the field corner and gap. Through this turn right along the field edge to Manor Cottage. Turn right then left past the buildings and continue on a defined path along the righthand perimeter of the field. Upon reaching the housing estate, bear left along the road which swings to your right to the A60 road and footpath sign—Steetley 2 miles. Turn left along Newcastle Avenue (A57) road. At the traffic lights in the centre of Worksop, continue ahead into Newcastle Street. And ahead at the next junction into Memorial Avenue with the car park on your left.

PRIORY CHURCH—dedicated to Our Lady and St. Cuthbert. The church was rebuilt in 1103 and has an exceptional Norman nave and the Lady Chapel is late 12th century. The gatehouse is the only one in England with a wayside shrine and chapel; it was built in 1314.

CHESTERFIELD CANAL—opened in 1777 and ran from Chesterfield to the river Trent and was designed by James Brindley. Today only the section from Worksop to the Trent is navigable. The section towards Chesterfield is popular with fisherman.

MANOR LODGE—Elizabethan building designed by Robert Smythson in the late 16th century. He also designed the Manor which was later destroyed by fire.

Chesterfield Canal in Worksop.

12

Archway House — Edwinstowe Walk.

Haughton Park House Farm — Walesby and Bothamsall Walk.

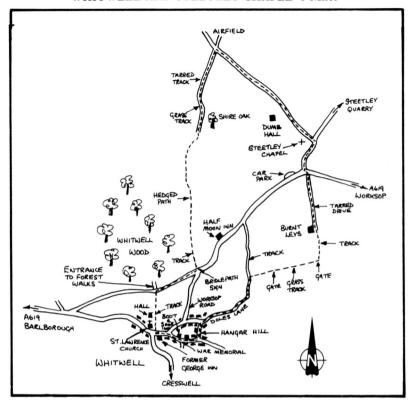

Steetley Church — Norman Doorway.

WHITWELL AND STEETLEY CHAPEL
—5 MILES—*allow 2½ hours.*

MAPS—O.S. 1:50,000 Sheet No 120—Mansfield and The Dukeries—O.S. 1:25,000 Sheet No SK47/57—Worksop (South) & Staveley

CAR PARK—no official one in Whitwell.
　　　　　—Parking at Steetley Chapel and at road junction beside the
　　　　　A619 road.

ABOUT THE WALK—Whitwell is an attractive unspoilt village rich in history, with Norman church and Elizabethan hall. You follow bridleways across the fields, with impressive views to Sherwood Forest, before passing close to the Shire Oak. Here the counties of South Yorkshire, Derbyshire and Nottinghamshire meet. The climax to the walk is Steetley Chapel, a truly exceptional Norman building. Whitwell Wood, which covers more than 400 acres has several walks in its domain. They are signed by coloured rings on posts—red for long, green for medium and yellow for short.

WALKING INSTRUCTIONS—I have started the walk from Whitwell parish church, dedicated to St.Lawrence, but being circular you can start anywhere. Walk up the track on the righthand side of the church, passing Whitwell Hall on your left. Upon reaching the A619 road, turn right. Infront of you is the entrance to Whitwell Wood and walks there. Walk beside the A619 road for ¼ mile to the junction with the B6043 Whitwell road. Turn left, as bridlepath signed and walk along the hedged track. This later becomes a magnificent hedged path. Just over a mile on your right is the infant Shire Oak. Shortly afterwards the path becomes a grass track and then a tarmaced lane. Ahead can be seen the planes of Netherthorpe airfield. Upon reaching the single track road, turn right and walk along this for a mile, passing Dumb Hall on your right. Just before the road junction you reach Steetley Chapel on your right.

Turn right at the road junction and upon reaching the A619 road, cross it to your left and walk up the drive to Burnt Leys Farm. Walk around the lefthand side of it on a track and at the end of the track, turn right through the metal gate and walk along the field boundary on a grass track. Just past some water troughs on your left you reach the end of the field. The path is now faint, but simply continue ahead across the field to a track. Turn left and follow this twisting lane into Doles Lane and Whitwell. Turn left down Hangar Hill and right at the bottom to gain the War Memorial. Continue ahead up High Street, past the aptly named Boot and Shoe Inn. With a village pump on your right, bear left along the road back to Whitwell church.

WHITWELL—The church dates back to Norman times with additions in the 14th and 15th century. Inside are several monuments, including one to Sir Roger Manners, a son of Dorothy Vernon of Haddon Hall. He lived nearby Whitwell Hall. Just east of the church is the former George Inn, with the iron work of the hanging sign still in place.

STEETLEY CHAPEL—Quite simply this is one of the finest Norman chapel's in the country. Overall it measures 52 feet long by 16 feet wide. But it has not always been in such a well preserved state. Over a hundred years ago it was a roofless building, but retoration began in 1875.

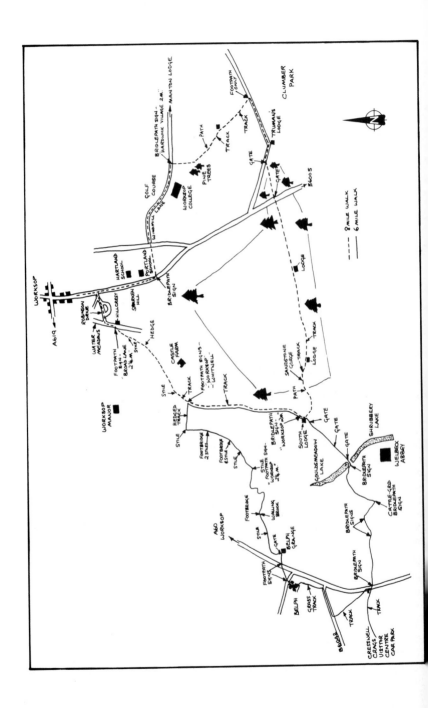

WELBECK
—6, 8 and 14 MILES—*allow 2½, 3½, or 6 hours*

MAPS—O.S. 1:50,000 Sheet No 120—Mansfield and The Dukeries—O.S. 1:25,000 Sheet No SK 47/47—Worksop (south) & Stavely—O.S. 1:25,000 Sheet No SK 67/77—Clumber Park and East Markham

CAR PARKS—Worksop—Close to Town Hall in Newgate Street.
　　　　　　　—Cresswell Crags Visitor's Centre.

ABOUT THE WALK—The 8 mile walk from Worksop passes through some of the finest woodland in England, and I make no apology for including this long walk, for it is magnificent. The 6 mile walk from Cresswell Crags takes you into the Welbeck Estate giving glimpses of the Abbey and lakes. Both walks provide views of Worksop Manor. The 14 mile walk that links the two shorter ones is an all day walk, through the essence of Dukeries walking—fields, woodland and impressive mansions.

WALKING INSTRUCTIONS—THE 8 MILE WALK—From the Town Hall in Worksop walk southwards along the B6005 road—Park Street. After ¼ mile turn right into Robinson Drive. Follow to the junction with Water Meadows road, and turn left. A few yards later and opposite the house named 'Hillcrest', turn right onto the footpath signposted—Broad Lane 2¼ miles. First you cross the bypass before walking along the fields perimeter, with the hedge on your immediate left. Far to your right is Worksop Manor and later on your left is the aptly named Castle Farm. Keep to the field edge for a mile to a stile, after which it becomes a track to a crossroads of paths and tracks beside a footpath sign for Worksop. Keep straight ahead on the track (the one your right is signposted Whitwell and is the one you follow on the 6 mile Cresswell Crag circuit.) After ½ a mile you enter woodland and a further ½ mile brings you to South Lodge and path sign—Worksop 2 miles.

Turn left and follow the well defined path/track for just over 2 miles through the forest to the B6005 road. After ½ mile you walk through a sandstone gorge; ¼ mile later pass a lodge and another ¾ mile later. At the road cross over to a gate and continue through the forest for almost ½ mile to another road. Turn right to Truman Lodge, an entrance into Clumber Park. Bear left along the road and under ½ mile later, left back into the forest, and follow a track to a house, ½ a mile away. Turn left and walk through the final part of the forest into fields, following a well defined path, which at the end of the second field, you reach a bridlepath through pine trees to a road on the righthandside of Worksop College. The bridlepath sign here states, Hardwick Village 2 miles.

Turn left and walk past Worksop College. Later you pass a golf course on your right, as you walk along Windmill Lane. At the road junction turn left then right and follow the bridlepath past the houses on your right. Upon reaching the B6005 road, turn right and ½ a mile later, after passing Portland and Hartland Schools on your right, you reach your starting out route.

WALKING INSTRUCTIONS—6 MILE ROUTE—From the car park at Cresswell Crags walk along the track away from the Visitor's Centre. At the A60 road cross over and walk along the road into Welbeck Estate, signposted—Bridlepath. ½ mile later at Oaksetts Lodge bear left onto concrete road, again bridlepath signed. Cross a minor road, again bridlepath signed, and 250 yards later at a cattle-grid, turn left onto a track and walk round the edge of two plantations, with playing fields in

17

the middle. The next ½ mile is well bridlepathed signed, as you bear right then left on a tarmaced road to reach the bridge inbetween Gouldsmeadow Lake and Shrubbery Lake.

Cross the bridge to a gate and walk up the field on a defined track to a gate halfway. At the end of the field reach trees and a large metal gate. close to South Lodge. Here the 8 mile route joins your route. Bear left then right onto the bridlepath signposted Worksop—2 miles. For almost ¾ mile you walk through forest, heading due north; a further ½ mile along the track in open country you reach a cross roads of paths. Turn left along the track signposted—Whitwell. At the end of the field turn left over the stile and walk along the righthandside of the field for 150 yards and turn right crossing two stiles, and a footbridge beside a wooden enclosure. Pass under the electric poles in the middle of the field to reach the far righthand corner of the field, where there is a footbridge and stiles. This path is not used a great deal but all the stiles are there. At the end of the field you reach two footpath signs—Worksop 2¼ miles and Belph 1¼ miles, your destination.

Continue ahead across the first field before bearing left in the next to the lefthand side of the field. At the end of the field the pathline goes directly across the field to the righthand side of a plantation but there is little evidence on the ground. It is better to bear left and walk around the fields perimeter to gain the plantation edge and footbridge. Across the next field you reach a stile before walking round the righthandside of the next field to a gate beside Belph Grange. Walk down the farm track to the road—A60—to a gate and footpath sign. Cross the road to a gate and cross the field to your left to a footbridge and path sign.

Cross the road and walk past the houses of Belph. At the road junction, turn left and follow the grass track to a minor road. Turn right and walk along the road, which can be avoided by a path on your right. After ¼ mile turn left and walk along a track to the A60 road. Turn right and you reach your starting out path. Turn right and walk along the track back to car park and Visitor's Centre.

WELBECK ABBEY—is private and can be glimpsed as you walk along the brideway. The buildings are now used by Welbeck College but are the work of the Dukes of Portland. Everything is on a grand scale; the riding school for instance, measures 385 feet long by 112 feet wide.

WORKSOP MANOR—The present building is Palladian but the original was designed by Robert Smythson. For a while the Shrewsbury family owned it and the 6th Earl together his wife Bess of Hardwick were guardians of the captive, Mary Queen of Scots. She stayed at the Manor twice in 1570. In 1761 a major fire destroyed the 500 room house. The present building was built soon afterwards.

Worksop Manor.

Welbeck: South Lodge.

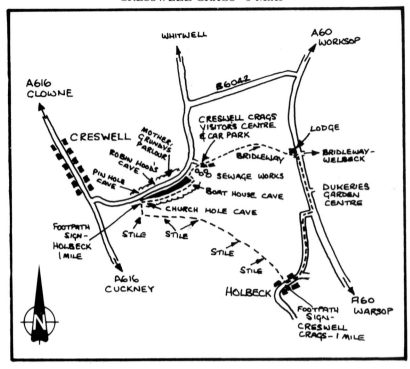

Welbeck College sign.

CRESSWELL CRAGS
—3 MILES—*allow 1½ hours*

CAR PARK—Cresswell Crags Visitor's Centre.

MAPS—O.S. 1:50,000 Sheet No 120—Mansfield and The Dukeries—O.S. 1:25,000 Sheet No SK47/57—Worksop (south) & Staveley.

ABOUT THE WALK—Cresswell Crags is a major site of palaeontology and the caves in the limestone gorge have revealed extremely important finds. A display and basic understanding of the site can be appreciated in the Visitor's Centre. Running through the gorge is the county boundary, with the northern caves inside Derbyshire and the southern in Nottinghamshire. The walk takes you through the gorge before crossing the fields to the hamlet of Holbeck. A short road walk past the entrance of the Dukeries Garden Centre returns you to the bridlepath back to the car park.

WALKING INSTRUCTIONS—Walk past the Visitor's Centre and turn left down the path with the sewage works on your left. Bear left around Crags Pond on a well defined path, passing the barred caves on your left. At the end of the lake, turn left, as footpath signposted—Holbeck 1 mile. First you ascend to a stile and vantage point before bearing left to a stile over the brow of the field. The wooded top of Cresswell Crags is on your left. The path is clear as you cross to another stile in the lefthand corner of the field before bearing right to the next. You keep close to field boundary on your left as you cross the stiled fields to Holbeck.

Turn left and follow the minor road to the A60 road, little over ¼ mile away. Turn left along the pavement passing the Dukeries Garden Centre on your right. Shortly afterwards and in front of a lodge, turn left onto the bridlepath, which as signposted to your right leads into Welbeck. Follow the track through the trees back to the Visitor's Centre and car park.

Cresswell Crags.

CRESSWELL CRAGS—The limestone gorge is the border of Derbyshire and Nottinghamshire, and the nearby Visitor's Centre is a joint project of both councils. The gorge has yielded some of the finest examples of fossils for the study of prehistoric man and man's evolution. The centre has a display of finds of Stone Age man.

21

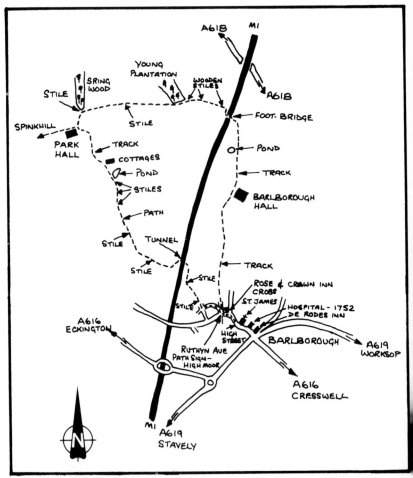

Park Hall.

22

BARLBOROUGH—4 MILES—*allow 2 hours.*

MAPS—O.S. 1:50,000 Sheet No 120—Mansfield and The Dukeries—O.S. 1:25,000 Sheet No SK47/57—Worksop (south) & Staveley

CAR PARK—no official one in Barlborough.

ABOUT THE WALK—Barlborough and its immediate area is particularly rich in historical buildings. First you see an 18th century hospital before the impressive church and nearby cross. Next you walk along a lane and pass the 16th century Barlborough Hall. Beyond you step into the 20th century and cross the M1 motorway and cross the fields to Park Hall. You return to Barlborough via tracks and field paths, where there are several inns.

WALKING INSTRUCTIONS—Walk along High Street in Barlborough, passing the former 18th century hospital and parish church, dedicated to St. James on your right. Shortly after pass the cross and Rose & Crown Inn also on your right. Just after turn right into Ruthyn Avenue as footpath signposted—High Moor. Keep straight ahead on the track and not the road which curves to your left. You soon leave the village behind and walk along a fenced track with distant views. After ½ mile pass Barlborough Hall on your right. Continue on the track and pass a small pond on your left. Beyond you can see the impressive footbridge over the M1. Leave the track and cross the bridge.

On the other side bear right on the path to a stile. Turn left and keep the field boundary on your left and cross the fields to a young plantation on your right, three fields away. The path is defined and well stiled. Beyond the far end (western) side of the plantation the path crosses the field and is defined. Over the brow you see the next stile. At the end of the next field you gain a further stile with Spring Wood on your immediate right. Turn left to the buildings of Park Hall and farm. At the track Park Hall is on your right. Turn left and follow the track as it descends to a small pond on your left. Immediately after leave the track for the stile and path. Ascend through the trees to another stile. Continue ascending gently to your right to another stile where the defined path hugs the field boundary on your right. After the next stile don't descend to the stream but bear left to a stile and follow the clear path round to the M1 motorway and a tunnel. Walk through this and turn right over the stile and walk beneath the motorway to the next stile. Just after turn left and ascend the field to a stile in the top lefthand corner. Ascend between the houses to Ruthyn Avenue and turn left to regain your starting out route.

BARLBOROUGH HALL—Built in 1584 and designed by Robert Smythson, who later designed Hardwick Hall. There is a strong resemblance between the two. The hall is now a school.

Barlborough Hall.

23

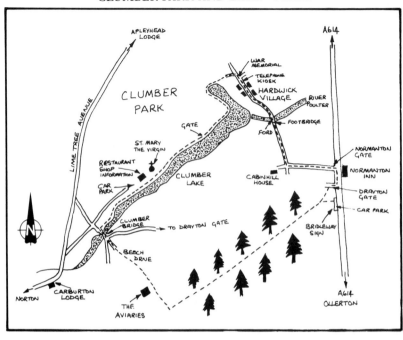

Clumber Bridge.

24

CLUMBER PARK AND LAKE
—6 MILES—*allow 3 hours*

MAPS—O.S. 1:50,000 Sheet No 120—Mansfield and The Dukeries—O.S. 1:25,000 Sheet No SK 67/77—Clumber Park and East Markham.—National Trust—Clumber Park—map and guide.

CAR PARK—Mansion House site—close to public conveniences and Information Centre. There are others in the Park and close to the perimeter of the park.

ABOUT THE WALK—Clumber Park is one of the finest Country Parks in Britain and owned by the National Trust. This walk encircles the southern half, to bring you to many of the key features —Clumber Bridge, the Lake and its wildfowl, woodland, Hardwick Village, Clumber Chapel and site of the Mansion House. There is an inn halfway round!

WALKING INSTRUCTIONS—From the car park walk to the lake and turn right along the path beside it. A little over ¼ mile later reach Clumber Bridge. Turn left and cross the bridge and take the middle road—straight ahead—and walk up the gently ascending track, known as Beech Drive. Keep on this for ¾ mile, passing far to your right, after ½ a mile, the Aviaries. Upon reaching a prominent T junction in the tracks, ¼ mile later, turn left and keep on this track for the next 1½ miles. Ignore all side tracks. In time you hear the A614 road and by the time you see it the track has deteriorated to a path. Follow it to your left to road in front of Drayton Gate. Turn right to the A614 road and turn left.

100 yards later, and just before the Normanton Inn, turn left and re-enter Clumber Park via Normanton Gate. The map shows a right of way from here across the field to your right towards Hardwick Village, but does not exist on the ground. Instead keep on the road and turn right and descend the road to the ford and footbridge over the Poulter River. Cross and walk through Hardwick Village. On the outskirts and just past a War Memorial on your right, turn left and descend the road to the Lake. Where the road leaves the lakeside, keep ahead on a track before turning left on a path and walking close to the bankside of the lake all the way back to the car park, Clumber Chapel and Mansion House site, a little over a mile away.

CLUMBER PARK—The 4,000 acre park was originally the home of the Duke Of Newcastle. The fifth Duke in the mid 18th century planted the double lime tree avenue—Duke's Drive—and at a mile long is the longest double lime avenue in Europe. 100 years ago the house was extensive, as can be seen by the outline near the Visitor's Centre. A major fire in 1897 destroyed many old rooms. In 1938 the house contents were sold and the estate became part of the National Trust. The chapel took three years to build and was completed in 1889 and designed by G.F. Bodley. The Clumber Bridge was built at the end of the 18th century.

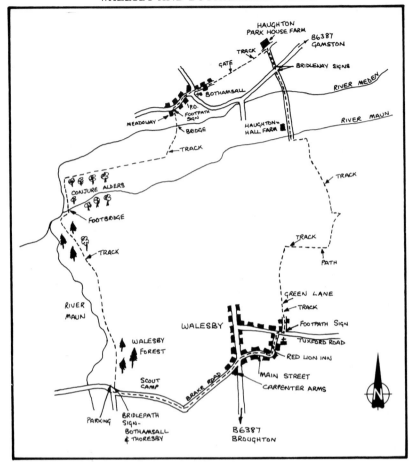

Bothamsall Church.

BOTHAMSALL—The attractive village has won the Best Kept Village competition for a population under 300. The church is largely 19th century. At Conjure Alders the rivers Maun and Meden run as one and are both crossed by footbridges. The route to them dates from Saxon times and the river was forded at a ford named Coningswath.

WALESBY AND BOTHAMSALL
—7 MILES—*allow 3 hours*

MAPS—O.S. 1:50,000 Sheet No 120—Mansfield and The Dukeries—O.S. 1:25,000 Sheet No SK 67/77—Clumber Park and East Markham

CAR PARK—no official one in Walesby or Bothamsall.
      —parking space beside path and road junction
      at Grid Ref: 665704

ABOUT THE WALK—The walk encircles a particularly attractive area with rolling wooded hills, unspoilt villages, secluded rivers and woodland. The walk is one of my favourite ones in this book. For ease of description I have begun the walk in Walesby but, being circular you can start it anywhere.

WALKING INSTRUCTIONS—Walk along the Main Street in Walesby past the Post Office and after following the road round to your left, past the Red Lion Inn. At the road junction beyond, turn right into Tuxford Road, and the parish church on your right. Turn left almost immediately into Green Lane; footpath signposted. Continue ahead past the houses and follow the hedged track. Later this becomes just a track along the field edge. After less than ½ mile at a crossroads of bridleways, keep ahead on the track which soon turns sharp right, as you follow a path along the righthand edge of the field. At the end of the field turn left, still keeping the field boundary on your right. In the hedge/trees is Bevercotes Beck. At the top end of the field gain a track and turn left along this. Almost immediately this turns sharp right as you follow the track through the righthand edge of a wood before open fields. ½ mile later reach a track junction and turn left then right over the River Maun onto a gravelled farm track, passing Haughton Hall Farm on your left. Pass under the railway line, cross the River Meden and reach the B6387 road. As bridlepathed signed continue ahead up the track to Haughton Park House Farm. Infront of the building turn left and follow the track to Bothamsall, a little over ½ a mile away.

Enter the village beside the church and continue ahead on the road, passing the Post Office. 150 yards later turn left onto a track, footpath signposted, beside the house—Meadoway. Follow the track over the River Meden and tributary before bearing right along the track to reach the trees of Conjure Alders, ½ mile away. Upon reaching the River Meden turn left along the track with the wood on your left and river on your right. Cross the footbridge over the River Maun and turn right and at the next footbridge, 50 yards later, left on a well defined path then track through Blackcliffe Hill Plantation. Less than ½ mile later you reach a junction of tracks at the wood's perimeter, keep right and follow the track beside the wood's perimeter. Soon you reach open country with the River Maun on your right and a small sandstone cliff. Continue ahead on the wide track keeping the trees of Walesby Forest on your left and reach the minor road beside the bridlepath sign—Bothamsall and Thoresby. Turn left and follow the road round to your left, past the Scout Camp and over the railway line. Follow the road round to your left—now Brake Road—and enter Walesby. Upon reaching the B6387 road beside the Carpenters Arms, cross over to the Main Street directly ahead.

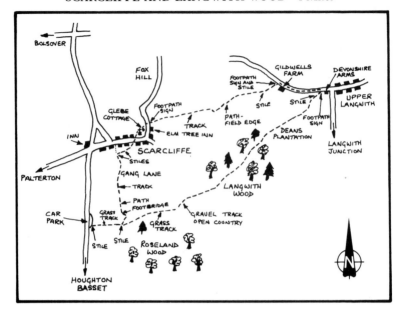

Scarcliffe Church.

SCARCLIFFE AND LANGWITH WOOD
—4 MILES—*allow 2 hours*

MAPS—O.S. 1:50,000 Sheet No 120—Mansfield and The Dukeries O.S. 1:25,000 Sheet No SK 46/56—Mansfield (North) and part of Sherwood Forest.

CAR PARK—lay-by beside 'Mansfield Road', ½ mile south of Scarcliffe at Grid Ref: 490679.

ABOUT THE WALK—a short walk through an unspoilt village whose church has a fascinating legend. Much of the walk is in quiet and attractive woodland on well defined paths and tracks. The added bonus is an inn at the halfway point! I may be biased but out of all the walks in this book, this one is my favourite.

WALKING INSTRUCTIONS—Ascend the stile beside the car park and walk along a grass track to a stile and trees of Roseland Wood.The track in front of you is your return path. Turn left and follow the path around the field boundary on your left to a footbridge. Cross this and enter Birch Hill Plantation. Keep right and walk up the righthand side of the plantation; at first on a path and later a track—Gang Lane. Just before reaching Scarcliffe village turn right over a stile and walk along the edge of the field to another wooden stile. Turn left over this and enter the village opposite the church. Walk into the churchyard following the path around the church on the left to reach a stile on the left of Glebe Cottage. Cross the playing field beyond to the minor road. Cross this and walk up the track, signposted—Public Footpath. The track is well defined for ½ a mile where it ends. Beyond it is a defined path along the field boundary on your left. At the end of the field is a stile and you descend to the minor road, near Gildwells Farm. Turn right and walk along the road for ¼ mile. Just before the Devonshire Arms Inn turn right onto a track and signposted footpath.

Keep on this track for little over one mile; first beside woodland before walking through Langwith Wood. Upon reaching a gravel track turn left along it into open country. 150 yards later turn right onto a grass track and continue in open country to a stile and entrance into Roseland Wood. Continue ahead and under ¼ mile later reach the stile you used at the beginning. Ascend this and retrace your steps along the grass track back to the car park.

SCARCLIFFE CHURCH—Inside is a tomb to Lady Constantia de Frecheville who died in about 1200 AD. She is holding a baby and according to tradition the following tale is told. After giving birth to a child her lover refused to marry her. She fled into Scarcliffe Wood but lost her way in the dense foliage. It was only by hearing the Curfew Bell being tolled at Scarcliffe Church that she found her way out of the forest, saving both herself and her baby's life. In her will she left five acres of land to pay for the Curfew Bell to be rung for six weeks each year, for ever. The bell has not been rung since the last war.

BOLSOVER, HARDWICK AND SUTTON SCARSDALE—12 Miles

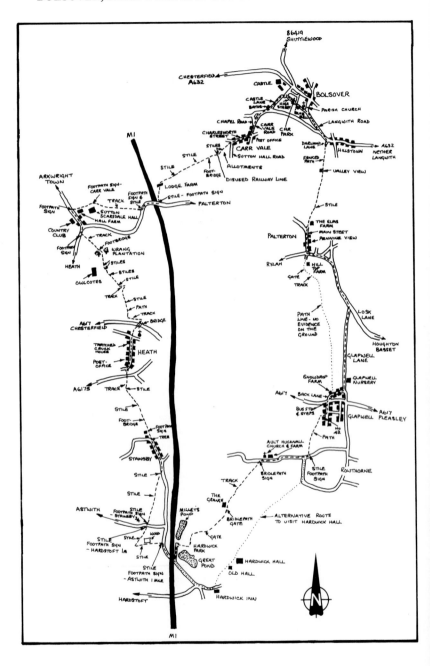

BOLSOVER CASTLE, HARDWICK HALL AND SUTTON SCARSDALE
—12 MILES—*allow 5 to 6 hours.*

MAPS—O.S. 1:50,000 Sheet No 120—Mansfield and The Dukeries—O.S. 1:25,000 Sheet No SK47/57—Worksop (south) & Staveley—O.S. 1:25,000 Sheet No SK46/56—Mansfield (North) and part of Sherwood Forest

CAR PARKS—Central Bolsover, beside Cotton Street
  —Hardwick Hall
  —Hardwick Park

ABOUT THE WALK—The longest walk in the book but one that links three of the finest buildings in England together. I first walked the route in the 1960's and since then it has become one of my favourite walks in eastern Derbyshire. The walk lies outside the accepted 'Dukeries' area but is very much part of the Ducal theme and the owners of the buildings were very much involved in the history of the Dukeries. It has never ceased to amaze me why this area is not walked more, for you encircle a stunning vale. It is for this reason that some of the paths are little used— the signs and stiles are all there. The only section with very little evidence on the ground is between Palterton and Glapwell. It may well be better to road walk round; about 1½ miles. Don't be put off; explore for yourself this area and enjoy the setting of the buildings and allow extra time visit them.

WALKING INSTRUCTIONS—From the car park in Cotton Street turn right, past the Information Office in the Library on your left. At the top of the road, with the Pentecostal Church on your left, turn left into High Street, with the Blue Bell Inn on your right. Walk past the parish church on your left to reach Langwith Road. Turn right along it and ¼ mile later at the first lefthand bend continue ahead into Darwood Lane. Almost immediately this becomes a fenced path with the houses on your left. After ¼ mile pass Valley View on your right and gain open country, with views and a defined path towards Palterton across the fields. At the first stile bear right following a grass track to walk round the righthand side of The Elms Farm to reach Main Street in Palterton. Continue ahead, past the aptly named house, Pennine View, to the road junction with Rylah Hill on your right. Ahead is the right of way past Hill Top Farm and along the vale edge to Glapwell, but there is little evidence on the ground. It is better to turn left along the road and take the first road on your right. ½ mile later turn right and walk along Glapwell Lane to Glapwell.

Just after passing Glapwell Nursery on your left turn right into Back Lane and follow this to the A617 road. On the way pass Snowdrop Farm where the right of way from Palterton comes out. Cross the A617 road to your right to the bus stop and steps. Ascend these and follow the path into Lime Tree Avenue. Turn right at house No. 42 and walk between the houses to the path across the fields to Ault Hucknall—this path is well defined. At the end of the second field reach the road (Ault Hucknall Lane) and turn right. ½ mile later pass the farm and Ault Hucknall church on your right. Just beyond turn left, at the bridlepath sign, and walk along the track to The Grange ½ mile away. If you want to visit Hardwick Hall instead of walking along the road to the church, turn left and follow the signposts to Hardwick Hall. From there you can descend to the Hardwick Inn and follow the road to your right to join the route at the M1 underpass.

From The Grange walk through the bridlepath gate and follow the defined path through the estate to another gate. Continue across the next field on the path to the gate and bridlepath sign close to the Great Pond. Bear right down the track through the wood and past quarries on your right to the National Trust Information building and car park. Turn left along the drive to the road and turn right to pass under the M1. About 150 yards later leave the road and ascend to a wooden stile beside the path sign—Astwith 1 mile. Keep to the edge of the field and pass a small wood on your right to a stile. In the next field continue ahead for 50 yards before turning sharp right to a stile in the middle of the hedge. Over this bear to your left to the field corner where there is another path sign—Hardstoft 1 mile—and stile. Cross the road to the next stile and path sign—Stainsby ¾ mile. Keep to the field edge as you walk beside a small plantation, ascending a stile on the way before descending to a stile and road on the outskirts of Stainsby. Continue ahead bearing left into Stainsby village.

Where the road turn sharp left, with a solitary tree on your right, turn right along the road to the school. At the building keep ahead to the stile and path sign—Heath ¾ mile. Descend the field to a footbridge and ascend with the field boundary on your right to a stile. Continue ahead in the next field with the fence on your left and at the top of the field the stile is on your right. Ascend this and gain the farm track, turning right. Cross the minor road and walk into Heath continuing ahead along the main street, past the Post Office and thatched cruck house on your left. Just afterwards where the road turns sharp left, continue ahead down a track and large foot/cattle bridge over the A617 road. Turn left down the track and at the bottom right following a path across the field to a stile. Ascend beyond along the field edge to a wood on your right. At the top of the field turn left onto a track and 30 yards later right over a stile. Cross the field diagonally to your left to a stile. Beyond are two more before reaching the track from Owlcotes. Cross over to the next stile and descend to Wrang Plantation with the fence on your right. At the plantation bear left through it to a footbridge and left after it to a pylon. Here you join a track up the field edge to a stile and footpath sign beside the road. Turn right then left into Sutton Scarsdale. Just after passing the Country Club on your left turn right, as footpath signposted, and walk down into Hall Farm.

Continue ahead on the track to pass the ruins of Sutton Scarsdale Hall on your right. As footpath signposted—Carr Vale—keep on the righthand track. ½ mile later gain Palterton Lane. Turn left and follow the road over the M1 and turn left at the stile and footpath sign. Walk along the track to the ruins of Lodge Farm. Pass through the archway and turn right following the defined path to a stile. Cross the next field diagonally to your left to a stile and beyond to a footbridge over the stream. The path is now very well defined as you cross the old railway line. Turn half left immediately to a stile and follow a path to another stile and track between the allotments to enter Carr Vale. Cross a minor track to reach Sutton Hall Road. Turn left then right along Charlesworth Street. At the end left into Carr Vale Road. You begin to ascend and ¼ mile later turn left at the Baths and ascend the steep Castle Lane. Follow it all the way to Castle Street. At the first bend a footpath on your left goes round underneath the castle grounds. If you keep ahead on Castle Street you will come to the entrance of the castle. By walking to your right you reach the car park on your left.

BOLSOVER CASTLE—a castle here dates back to Norman times but the present Keep dates from the early 17th century. The principal owner when the Keep, Long Gallery, and Riding Stables were built in the early 17th century was Sir William Cavendish, who later became the Earl of Mansfield and Duke of Newcastle. The Royalists and Parliamentarians occupied the building and was seized by Parliament

The Keep — Bolsover Castle.

in 1644. In 1755 it came into the possession of the Dukes of Portland but much of it was stripped for use at Welbeck Abbey. In 1945 the partially ruined buildings were given to the then Ministry of Works, now the Ministry for the Enviroment, and it is they who look after the buildings and are carrying out an extensive restoration programme.

HARDWICK HALL—one of the finest Elizabethan buildings in Britain and often referred to as 'more glass then wall'. The occupier was the renowned Bess of Hardwick, the wife of George Talbot the sixth Earl of Shrewsbury. Work began in 1590 and seven years later she took up residence. The interior contains an extensive range of tapestries and well known for its plasterwork in the Great Chamber and Long Gallery. The building is basically unaltered and each tower carries the bold initials ES— Elizabeth Shrewsbury. The building remained in the Cavendish family (the current Dukes of Devonshire) until 1959 when it was accepted in lieu of Death Duties and given to the National Trust.

SUTTON SCARSDALE HALL—now a magnificent ruin but was built by the fourth Earl of Scarsdale in 1780.

Hardwick Hall.

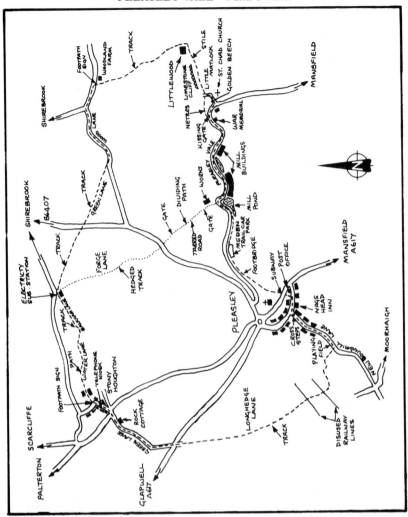

Robin Hood's Way Sign.

PLEASLEY VALE—4 MILES AND 8 MILES
—allow 2 or 4 hours

MAPS—O.S. 1:50,000 Sheet No 120—Mansfield and The Dukeries O.S. 1:25,000 Sheet No SK46/56—Mansfield (North and part of Sherwood Forest.

CAR PARK—Meden Trail car park, near Pleasley Vale. Grid Ref: 551649.

ABOUT THE WALK—Encircling Pleasley and Vale are a whole series of green lanes which provide level walking. Sandwiched between coal mines of Shirebrook and Pleasley, the area is full of contrast from farming country, mines, woodland, rivers and mill ponds, outcrops of rock and mill complexes. This walk encompasses all and can either be done as a long 8 mile route or as two separate walks of about 4 miles each. The walk uses part of the Meden Trail which runs from Pleasley to Woodhouse—1¾ miles long.

WALKING INSTRUCTIONS—Leave the car park via its eastern end, following the path towards Pleasley Vale. The path weaves its way near the stream on your right, past sluice gates to a large mill pond. Shortly afterwards gain the road and turn right to enter the mill complex of Pleasley Vale. Just before you enter the complex on your left is the tarmaced path which cuts the whole circuit in half. If you are doing a shorter walk, use this. The first ½ mile is tarmaced to the B6407 road. On the otherside you follow a track; grass at first but later a rough surface to reach the main route beside an electrical sub station, close to the Shirebrook road. The main route comes in from your right—Forge Lane, and continues you to your left via Balkham Lane and Water Lane to Stony Houghton.

Walk along the road past the mills and ponds of Pleasley Vale. Shortly after the War Memorial on your right, the road turns right. On the corner on your left is a white kissing gate and path. This leads you into an area known as Little Matlock. The path in the summer is heavily nettled and can be avoided by following the road round to a road on your left beside a copper beech tree. Turn left along this and at St. Chad's church left and cross the stream before turning right onto a well defined path. The nettled path comes in from your left here. The path is a delightful stretch of walking with limestone cliffs on your left and the stream on your right. At the second stile continue ahead on a track and follow it to your left passing the buildings of Littlewood on your left. Follow the track for almost a mile to a road junction on the outskirts of Shirebrook, beside a footpath sign.

Turn left and now follow Wood Lane, bearing left along it at a road junction, after 300 yards. A little over ¼ mile later pass the Forestry Commission entrance to Pleasley Park on your left. Just afterwards leave the road on your right and follow a wide track, known as Green Lane. After ½ mile cross the B6407 road (Common Lane) and follow the track for another ½ mile to the junction of lanes at the electricity sub station. Walk round the sub station to your left and the track of Balkham Lane. A further ½ mile brings you to delightful countryside—outcrops of rock and a shallow valley. Beyond the track becomes a path up Water Lane to Stony Houghton. Entering the village continue ahead to the main road in the village, beside a footpath sign, and turn left. Walk past the telephone kiosk and shortly afterwards at the B6417 keep straight ahead for a few yards before turning left and passing Rock Cottages on your left. Keep on this road for the next ½ mile—known as Green Lane—to the A617 road.

Go straight across the road and follow the tarmaced and later track of Longhedge Lane, which you follow for the next 1½ miles. On your left is Pleasley mine. Just after crossing the second disused railway line turn left and descend the track to Newboundmill Lane on the outskirts of Upper Pleasley. Turn left and follow this road for ½ mile past the houses to the road junction and cross steps. Turn right onto Chesterfield Road, passing the Nags Head Inn on your right. Shortly afterwards and before the Post Office, turn left and follow the path through the subway beneath the A617 road. Follow the wide path with the stream on your left. After ½ a mile cross the stream via a footbridge and follow the path back to the car park.

PLEASLEY VALE—Before the coming of the textile mills, iron forges were operating here in the 17th and 18th century. The first mill was built on the site of the forge in 1784. Further buildings were built but serious fires in 1840 and 1844 destroyed the original buildings. Shortly afterwards the mills—William Hollins & Co., Ltd.,—were rebuilt and are what we see today.

Pleasley Mill.

Pleasley Vale War Memorial.

Sherwood Forest sign.

Robin Hood.

Jousting in Sherwood Forest.

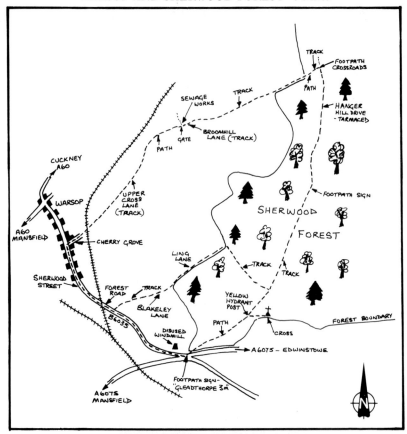

CUCKNEY A60

WARSOP

A60 MANSFIELD

SEWAGE WORKS

TRACK

TRACK

PATH

FOOTPATH CROSSROADS

HANGER HILL DRIVE - TARMACED

GATE

BROOMHILL LANE (TRACK)

PATH

UPPER CROSS LANE (TRACK)

CHERRY GROVE

SHERWOOD FOREST

FOOTPATH SIGN

LING LANE

SHERWOOD STREET

FOREST ROAD

TRACK

BLAKELEY LANE

TRACK

TRACK

B6035

YELLOW HYDRANT POST

PATH

CROSS

FOREST BOUNDARY

DISUSED WINDMILL

A6075 – EDWINSTOWE

FOOTPATH SIGN – "GLEADTHORPE 3m"

A6075 MANSFIELD

N

Cross on the site of St. Edwin's Chapel.

WARSOP AND SHERWOOD FOREST
—6 MILES—*allow 2½ hours*

MAPS—O.S. 1:50,000 Sheet No 120—Mansfield and The Dukeries—O.S. 1:25,000 Sheet No SK 46/56—Mansfield (North) and part of Sherwood Forest.

CAR PARK—no official one, but parking space at the crossroads the A6075/B6035 (Warsop road).

ABOUT THE WALK—The first half of the walk is through the diverse woodland of Sherwood Forest, along paths, tracks and tarred drive. En route you can make a side trip to see the site of St. Edwin's Chapel. The second half is along an excellent path beside the fields to the southern part of Warsop. A little over a mile of road walking returns you to the crossroads. The walk can be extended by a mile by walking along the track of Blakeley Lane and Ling Lane, to enter the forest again to return to the crossroads.

WALKING INSTRUCTIONS—From the crossroads follow the well defined path— signposted 'Gleadthorpe 3 miles'—and enter the forest. After ½ mile you pass a yellow hydrant concrete post on your left. To visit the cross marking the site of St. Edwin's Chapel, turn right and follow the path across a tarred drive and along a path close to the forest's perimeter. About 100 yards from the tarred drive on your right almost hidden by the trees is the cross; return the same way. A little over ¼ mile later you reach open country on your left and a gravel track (this is the track you walk up on your left if doing the mile extension from Blakeley Lane) continue ahead for the next mile.

At the footpath sign bear left and begin walking along the tarred surface of Hanger Hill Drive. Almost a mile later you reach a crossroads of paths/tracks beside path signs. Turn left on a track and where it swings left soon afterwards keep ahead on a defined path. This path keeps to the edge of Gleadthorpe New Plantation. ¼ mile later you leave the forest behind and begin walking along the edge of the fields (on your right) on a grass track. Little over ½ mile later reach a sewage works on your right. Where the lane—Broomhill Lane turns sharp right, continue ahead to a gate and and path. After two fields this becomes a well defined track. Ignore two tracks to your right; simply keep ahead and a mile later reach Cherry Grove and walk past the houses of Warsop. At the main road (B6035)—Sherwood Street —turn left and walk and begin walking out of Warsop. After walking under the railway the road name becomes Forest Road. Shortly afterwards is Blakeley Lane, with Scout Camp sign. As detailed on the map you can walk along the track back into the forest to join the early part of the route. Simply turn right upon reaching it and retrace your steps to the crossroads. If heading direct to the crossroads continue on Forest Road to the road junction ½ a mile away.

ST. EDWINS CHAPEL—Edwinstowe is named after Edwin, King of Northumbria. At the time of the Domesday Book in 1086 there was only a church, a priest and four bordars. The origin of the Chantry chapel dedicated to St. Edwin is unknown. The cross, erected by a Duke of Portland, is believed to be the site of the chapel.

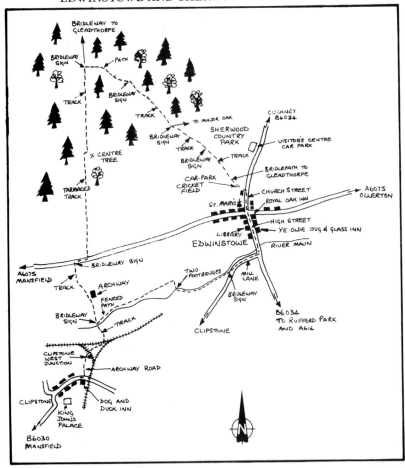

Bridleway Sign.

EDWINSTOWE AND SHERWOOD FOREST—St. Mary's church is said to be the place where Robin Hood and Maid Marion were betrothed. The nearby Visitor's Centre has an exhibition to Robin Hood. Paths from here lead to Major Oak, the hideout for Robin Hood and his men. Near Clipstone is the Duke's Archway, built by the 4th Duke of Portland in 1844. It is similar to the gatehouse of Worksop Priory. The niches have carved figures including Robin Hood. In Clipstone is the ruin of King John's Palace—a royal hunting lodge once in a deer park.

EDWINSTOWE AND SHERWOOD FOREST
—5 MILES—*allow 2½ hours*

MAPS—O.S. 1:50,000 Sheet No 120—Mansfield and The Dukeries—O.S. 1:25,000 Sheet No SK 66/76—Ollerton

CAR PARKS—beside cricket and fairground.—Sherwood Forest Visitor's Centre.

ABOUT THE WALK—Sherwood Forest and the story of Robin Hood are well known. Instead of walking to see Major Oak, this walk takes you into lesser walked areas of the forest and places in the vicinity of Edwinstowe which can only be reached on foot—the flood dyke, river Maun and a remarkable archway gatehouse. There are two side trips from the main route to visit Major Oak and Clipstone where there is an inn and ruins of King John's Palace. These two additions add on 1½ miles. You return to the car park via Edwinstowe with the opportunity of visiting the parish church.

WALKING INSTRUCTIONS—From the car park beside the cricket ground, cross the field to your left and upon reaching the forest edge pick up the wide path signposted—Bridlepath to Gleadthorpe. Keep on this track for ¼ mile to a junction of paths. As guided by the metal bridlepath sign bear left, but not sharp left, and continue along a wide track with a solitary wire fence on your immediate left. A further ¼ mile brings you to another junction. The path on your right goes to Major Oak, but again as signposted keep ahead on the track passing through pine and scattered oak woodland. A further ½ mile brings you to another path junction, with bridlepath sign. Take the left track which soon becomes a path as you bear left, heading due west.Little over ¼ mile later reach a T junction of tracks. Turn left and follow the wide track, now heading due south. Little over ½ mile brings you to a tarmaced junction close to the Centre Tree. Turn right then left and walk along the tarmaced surface through the trees to A6075 road, over ½ mile away.

Turn right and walk along the road for 200 yards to the track and bridlepath sign on your left. Turn left and follow this track, keeping to your right to reach the Archway ¼ mile away. Continue past the archway to the bridlepath sign on your left, for the path beside the Flood Dyke. From here you can make a side trip to Clipstone by continuing ahead on the track. After passing under the first railway bridge turn right and pass under another beside the Clipstone West Junction signal box. ¼ mile along the track—now Archway road brings you to the Dog and Duck Inn and in the field not far away are the reamins of King John's Palace. Retrace your steps back to the fenced path beside the Flood Dyke.

Follow this path for ½ mile. Just before reaching school playing fields and a sharp lefthand bend in the track, turn right and cross two footbridges and walk along the banks of the River Maun for almost ½ mile to Mill Lane. Continue ahead along the road and at the junction with the B6034 road turn left and keep straight ahead through Edwinstowe up the High Street, past the Library and Ye Olde Jug and Glass Inn to the road junction beside the Royal Oak Inn. Continue ahead on Church Street, passing the parish church dedicated to St. Mary on your left. A short distance more brings you to the road and car park beside the cricket field.

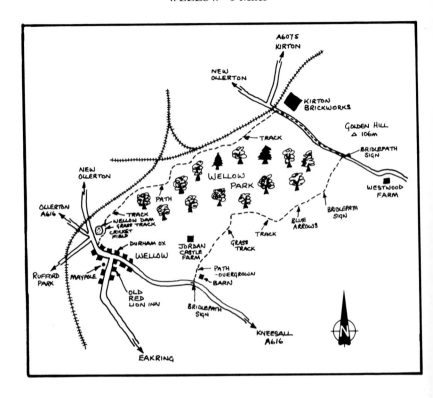

Wellow Dam.

WELLOW—5 MILES—*allow 2½hours*

MAPS—O.S. 1:50,000 Sheet No 120—Mansfield and The Dukeries—O.S. 1:25,000 Sheet No SK 66/76—Ollerton

CAR PARK—beside Wellow Dam.

ABOUT THE WALK—I hesitated to include this walk at first, simply because part of the route is overgrown and little walked. But upon reflection I thought it should be included for that reason, for all the path signs are there and it does pass through and encircle the woodland of Wellow Park. It is an area that should be walked in, and the village of Wellow is one of the most attractive in the area, with a small dam, green and maypole. I hope these notes don't deter you for it is an enjoyable walk which gives added satisfaction of walking if one has had to battle through a rather overgrown path. Perhaps a winter walk?

WALKING INSTRUCTIONS—From Wellow Dam, walk past it to a grass track on your left which keeps away from the dam and the cricket field on your right. The track soon becomes a hedged and well defined track as you approach the trees of Wellow Park, ¼ mile away. Upon entering the forest you keep to the northern perimeter of Wellow Park, following a well defined track—sometimes path—for the 1½ miles. Upon reaching the road—Ollerton to Laxton—beside the railway line on your left, turn right passing the entrance to the Kirton Brickworks on your left. Keep on the road for ½ mile.

Upon reaching Laxton Common, turn right at the Bridleway sign and follow the path across the field to the southern edge of Wellow Park. Shortly after entering the forest you reach a crossroads of bridleways. Bear right on the path keeping near the wood's perimeter, for the next mile. The pathline is defined but in summer a little overgrown in places. The whole route is well signed with blue arrowed posts at regular intervals. After almost a mile you leave the trees and walk along a wide grass track, which soon becomes a track. ¼ mile along here you reach gates on either side of the track. The one on the right is the track to Jordan Castle Farm. You keep straight ahead, as blue arrowed, and walk along the most overgrown section. A little over¼ mile later you reach the minor road—Wellow to Ompton . Turn right and walk into Wellow, passing the green and maypole on your left, the Durham Ox Inn on your right and just round the corner, Wellow Dam.

Wellow Maypole.

43

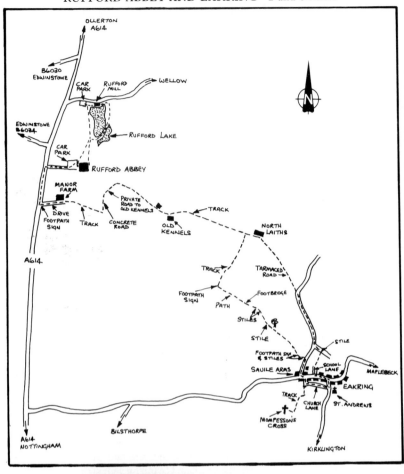

Savile Arms Sign, Eakring.

RUFFORD ABBEY AND EAKRING
—2 AND 8 MILES—*allow 1 or 3 hours*

MAPS—O.S. 1:50,000 Sheet No 120—Mansfield and The Dukeries—O.S. 1:25,000 Sheet No SK 66/76—Ollerton

CAR PARKS—Rufford Mill and Rufford Abbey—both parts of Rufford Country Park.

ABOUT THE WALK—A short 2 mile walk can be done from either car park to encircle Rufford Lake and explore the Abbey and gardens. The lake is a wildlife reserve with a variety of waterfowl to be seen including, coot, moorhen, mute swan, Canada geese, barnacle geese, great crested grebe,shelduck, heron, mallard, pochard and tufted duck. The principal walk is across the fields by tracks and path to the village of Eakring. The village is particularly attractive and rich in historical associations with William Mompesson, the former Rector of Eyam in Derbyshire during the plague there in 1665/6. The walk back from Eakring provides distant views over area and there is an inn in Eakring at the half-way point.

WALKING INSTRUCTIONS—Starting from the car park at Rufford Abbey, walk along the entrance drive to the A614 road. Turn left and ¼ mile later left again at footpath sign and walk along the drive to Manor Farm. Continue ahead past it on a track to a wood on your right. Keep ahead to a concrete track. Turn left and, shortly after passing a house on your right, turn right onto a 'Private Road to the Old Kennels.' Follow this as it sweeps round to your right and ½ mile later pass a house on your left. Continue ahead to the Old Kennels (now a modern house on your right). Past the house the concrete drive becomes a track and a little over ½ a mile approach the buildings North Laiths. Just before on your right is a track which you will be walking up on your return from Eakring.

Continue past North Laiths, now on a tarmaced lane, and in ½ mile reach the minor road towards Eakring. Turn right and walk along the road and upon reaching a sharp right hand bend at the Eakring sign, turn left onto a grass track. 50 yards along here turn right over the stile and ascend the field to another stile. Continue ahead into School Lane. Upon reaching the Main Street, turn left and right at Kirklington Road to Eakring church dedicated to St. Andrews. Turn right opposite into Church Lane, following the signs to Mompesson's Cross. Where the lane turns sharp right—you will return to here—turn left and follow the track to see Mompesson's Cross, ¼ mile away. Return the same way and walk down Church Lane to the Main Street.

Turn left then right into Wellow Road, passing the Savile Arms on your left. Pass the five storey mill tower on your right before leaving the road on your left at the stile and footpath sign. Reach another stile almost immediately before crossing the next to a track. Continue ahead over the next field passing a small plantation on your right, to a stile on the left. During the summer these two fields could be full of crops and the pathline not obvious. It is best to walk round the field's perimeter to reach the stiles.

Over the next stile the view unfolds and you descend to a bridge over the disused railway line. Beyond you cross another field to a footbridge. In the next field the path line is clearly defined as you head for a track and path sign. Turn right and walk along the track to the track close to North Laiths. Turn left and retrace your steps back to Rufford Abbey.

RUFFORD ABBEY—dates back to 1147 when the Cistercian abbey was built. There are ruins of an Elizabethan house, and extensive 19th century estate buildings. The estate is now a 175 acre country park and the buildings are used for a variety of uses; the Stables are now a craft centre. There are extensive gardens to explore and a delightful walk around the 25 acre Rufford Lake. The monks were here until 1536 when the estate was obtained by the 6th Earl of Shrewsbury, Bess of Hardwick's fourth husband. The tragic Lady Arabella Stuart was married here.Following the Earl's death the property passed into the Savile family who held the estate for the next 400 years. The contents of the house were sold in 1938 and the estate was later aquired by the Nottinghamshire County Council.

EAKRING—Following the plague in Eyam, Derbyshire, in 1665/6 when 287 people died, the Rector William Mompesson came to Eakring and worked here for 38 years until his death in 1708. A cross outside the village marks the place where he held his first service on arrival at Eakring. Near the western door of the church can be seen the gravestone to Edward Cartwright Senior Late Keeper to His Grace the Duke of Kingston 55 years. He died in 1773 aged '80 years 10 months and Three Weeks.' His epitaph reads—

> My Gun discharged my ball is gone
> My powder spent my work is done.
> Those panting Deer I have left behind
> May now have time to gain their wind
> Who I have ofttimes chased them O'er
> The Verdant Plains, but now no more

Mompesson Cross — Eakring.

Rufford Lake.

Rufford Abbey.

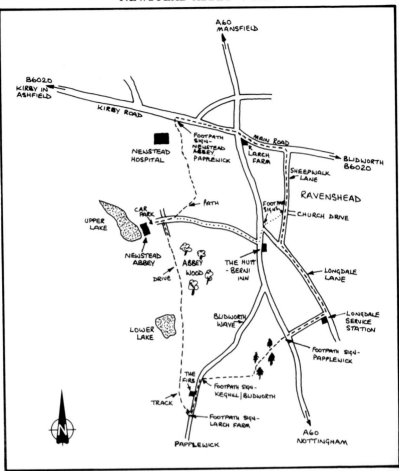

Newstead Abbey and Lake.

NEWSTEAD ABBEY—7 MILES—*allow 3 hours*

MAPS—O.S. 1:50,000 Sheet No 120—Mansfield and The Dukeries—O.S. 1:25,000 Sheet No SK45/55

CAR PARK—Newstead Abbey

ABOUT THE WALK—I first wrote about this walk fifteen years ago and it still remains one of the most pleasant in the region. With quiet lanes, extensive woodland and a fascinating Abbey and its historical associations with Lord Byron.

WALKING INSTRUCTIONS—Walk down the drive from the car park, the way you drove in. Keep ahead at the crossroads—the road on your right is the one you return on. 50 yards later on your left leave the road and follow the defined track through the trees. First you ascend before descending—now on a path—and leave the trees behind as you reach a large field. Keep on the righthand side of it along the path. Ahead is Newstead Hospital which you pass well to the right of. In the final stages the path becomes a fenced one as you reach the B6020 road beside path sign—Newstead Abbey, Papplewick, and Linby. Turn right and walk along Kirby Road. ½ mile later reach Larch Farm at the crossroads. Continue ahead on the Main Road and ¼ mile later turn right along Sheepwalk Lane. After ¾ mile join Longdale Lane and turn left along it. Before this road and opposite Church Drive you can turn right along a signposted path. This brings you out at the top of Longdale Road beside the Berni Inn—The Hutt. Opposite is the entrance to Newstead Abbey and the car park is a little over a mile away up the drive.

Walk along Longdale Lane to Longdale Service Station and turn right up the road to the A60 road. Go straight across and follow the signposted path—Paplewick and Linby. First you walk beside the field to a forest, pass through this to another before a further field brings you to the B683 road, beside the path sign—Keghill and Blidworth. Turn left along the road, passing The Firs and ½ mile later after descending a hill reach the path sign—Larch Farm—and walk along the track. This takes you past Lower Lake after a mile before Abbey Wood, now on a tarmaced drive. Follow this round to your left to reach the crossroads you passed at the start. Turn left back to the car park.

NEWSTEAD ABBEY—remains of the Priory Church can be seen built in 1170. In the 16th century—1540—it was changed into a mansion by the Byron family. Many items associated with Lord Byron can be seen.

Newstead Abbey.

49

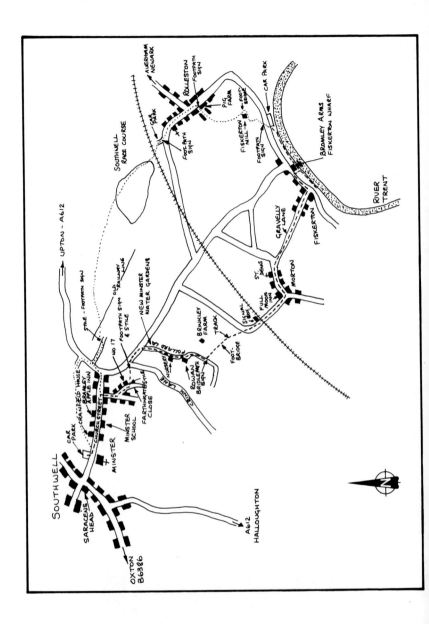

SOUTHWELL MINSTER—dates from 1108 with further work in the 13th century, especially the Chapter House in 1295 which is world renowned for its stone carvings, particularly the 'Leaves of Southwell''. Adjacent to the Minster are the ruins of the 15th century Archbishop's Palace.

SARACEN'S HEAD—where Charles Stuart spent his last hours as a free man before surrendering to the Scots at Kelham.

SOUTHWELL AND THE RIVER TRENT
—4 MILES one way—8 MILES return
—allow 4 hours

MAPS—O.S. 1:50,000 Sheet No 120—Mansfield and The Dukeries—O.S. 1:25,000 Sheet No SK 65/75

CAR PARK—Opposite Southwell Minster in Church Street.

ABOUT THE WALK—Southwell with its Minster and Saracen's Head is steeped in history. A walk around the streets will bring you to many magnificent buildings, such as Cranfield House in Church Street. I had planned a circular walk here but many of the rights of way are so little used that in summer it is like scything your way through a jungle in places. In the end I decided to make it a return walk and briefly detail the circular route from the River Trent, for those who wish to try. Despite this it is a magnificent walk along the lanes and over the fields to the River Trent at Fiskerton. The reward is an inn overlooking the river, where boats glide by and where there is a pleasant stroll along the river banks.

WALKING INSTRUCTIONS—Turn left out of the car park along Church Street, past Cranfield House, the Minster School and Bramley Apple Inn. Shortly afterwards turn right into Farthingate and left into Farthingate Close. At house No.17 turn left to stile and footpath sign. Walk up the field to the next stile and onto a track to gain the Fiskerton Road, with Crink Lane on your right. Walk along the Fiskerton Road to Pollard Lane, with the New Minster Water Gardens on your left. Walk along the lane for ½ mile passing Rowan House and bridlepath sign pointing along the track. At the next sign turn left and follow the bridlepath across the fields, passing Brinkley Farm well to your left, before crossing a footbridge. Ascend under the electric pylons, now on a track as you approach the road to Morton. Continue ahead past the signal box and hall into Morton. Turn left past the Full Moon Inn and, just after passing the parish church dedicated to St. Denis, turn right along Gravelly Lane to Fiskerton. Turn left at the road junction and 200 yards later reach Fiskerton Wharf and Bromley Arms. Return the same way back to Southwell.

For those doing the circular walk, walk along the river bank to your right to the fisherman's car park. Cross the road to a footpath sign and walk along the top of the dyke to the stile on your right and path to Fiskerton Mill. Walk past the mill to a stile on your left, beyond which is a footbridge. Continue along a dyke beside a river channel in woodland. At the next stile bear right away from the channel to reach Rolleston. Turn left along the road, keeping left at the junction to pass Rolleston Manor and church. Almost immediately afterwards turn right into the Race Course car park and footpath sign. Keep right to the wooden fence and door—signed path to Upton. You emerge onto the race course. It is best to cross it and and walk beside the track to the main curve. Cross the track picking up a footpath arrow and now walk along the field boundary with a water channel on your right. The pathline is now indistinct and hard to follow. Continue along the field perimeter past a house on your right and later a footbridge. Still keep to the field's edge for another ½ mile before turning left away from the channel to cross a disused railway line to gain a lane. Turn right and follow this to the A612 road. Here you can either turn left and follow it back to the Minster or continue ahead on the minor road and take the first road on your left and left again onto a path which will return you to near the Minster.

EQUIPMENT NOTES
—some personal thoughts

BOOTS—perferably with a leather upper, of medium weight, with a vibram sole. I always add a foam cushioned insole to help cushion the base of my feet.

SOCKS—I generally wear two thick pairs as this helps to minimise blisters. The inner pair of loop stitch variety and approximately 80% wool. The outer a thick rib pair of approximately 80% wool.

WATERPROOFS—for general walking I wear a T shirt or shirt with a cotton wind jacket on top. You generate heat as you walk and I prefer to layer my clothes to avoid getting too hot. Depending on the season will dictate how many layers you wear. In soft rain I just use my wind jacket for I know it quickly dries out. In heavy downpours I slip on a neoprene lined cagoule, and although hot and clammy it does keep me reasonably dry. Only in extreme conditions will I don overtrousers, much preferring to get wet and feel comfortable.

FOOD—as I walk I carry bars of chocolate, for they provide instant energy and are light to carry. In winter a flask of hot coffee is welcome. I never carry water and find no hardship from doing so, but this is a personal matter. From experience I find the more I drink the more I want. You should always carry some extra food such as Kendal Mint Cake for emergencies.

RUCKSACK—for day walking I use a climbing rucksac of about 40 litre capacity and although excess space it does mean that the sac is well padded and with a shoulder strap. Inside apart from the basics for the day I carry gloves, balaclava, spare pullover and a pair of socks.

MAP & COMPASS—when I am walking I always have the relevant map—usually 1:25,000 scale—open in my hand. This enables me to constantly check that I am walking the right way. In case of bad weather I carry a Silva type compass, which once mastered gives you complete confidence in thick cloud or mist.

Cranfield House — Southwell.

OTHER BOOKS BY JOHN N.MERRILL
& PUBLISHED BY JNM PUBLICATIONS

DAY WALK GUIDES

PEAK DISTRICT: SHORT CIRCULAR WALKS Fifteen carefully selected walks—3 to 5 miles—starting from a car park. The walks cover the variety of the area—the gritstone edges, limestone dales, and peat moorland. All follow well defined paths; include a pub for lunch; and are suitable for all the family. 44 pages 16 maps 32 photographs   ISBN 0 907496 16 4

PEAK DISTRICT TOWN WALKS Twelve short circular walks around the principal towns and villages of the Peak District. Including Castleton, Buxton, Hathersage, Eyam,Tissington and Ashbourne. Each walk has a detailed map and extensive historical notes complete with pictures. 60 pages 12 maps 96 photographs   ISBN 0 907496 20 2

PEAK DISTRICT: LONG CIRCULAR WALKS Fifteen differing walks 12 to 18 miles long for the serious hiker. Many follow lesser used paths in the popular areas, giving a different perspective to familiar landmarks. 64 pages 16 maps 28 photographs   ISBN 0 907496 17 2

WESTERN PEAKLAND—CIRCULAR WALKS The first book to cover this remarkably attractive side of the National Park—west of Buxton. The guide combines both long and short walks. 25 -3 to 11 mile long walks with extremely detailed maps to help you explore the area. 48 pages 23 maps 22 photographs
ISBN 0 907496 15 6

12 SHORT CIRCULAR WALKS AROUND MATLOCK 12 walks of about 4 miles long into the Matlock area rich in history and folklore and make ideal family outings. Included is an 'alpine' walk, using Matlock Bath's cable car as part of the route. 52 pages 44 photographs 12 maps   ISBN 0 907496 25 3

SHORT CIRCULAR WALKS IN THE DUKERIES More than 25 walks in the Nottinghamshire/Sherwood Forest area, past many of the historic buildings that make up the Dukeries area.   ISBN 0 907496 29 6

DERBYSHIRE AND THE PEAK DISTRICT CANAL WALKS More than 20 walks both short and long along the canals in the area—Cromford, Erewash, Chesterfield, Derby, Trent, Peak Forest and Macclesfield canals.
ISBN 0 907496 30 X

HIKE TO BE FIT: STROLLING WITH JOHN John Merrill's personal guide to walking in the countryside to keep fit and healthy. He describes what equipment to use, where to go, how to map read, use a compass and what to do about blisters! 36 pages 23 photos 2 sketches 3 charts   ISBN 0 907496 19 9

CHALLENGE WALKS

JOHN MERRILL'S PEAK DISTRICT CHALLENGE WALK A 25 mile circular walk from Bakewell, across valleys and heights involving 3,700 feet of ascent. More than 2,000 people have already completed the walk. A badge and completion certificate is available to those who complete. 32 pages 18 photographs 9 maps
ISBN 0 907496 18 0

JOHN MERRILL'S YORKSHIRE DALES CHALLENGE WALK A 23 mile circular walk from Kettlewell in the heart of the Dales. The route combines mountain, moorlands, limestone country and dale walking with 3,600 feet of ascent. A badge and certificate is available to those who complete the route. 32 pages 16 photographs 8 maps
ISBN 0 907196 28 8

THE RIVER'S WAY A two day walk of 43 miles, down the length of the Peak District National Park. Inaugurated and created by John, the walk starts at Edale, the end of the Pennine Way, and ends at Ilam. Numerous hostels, campgrounds, B&B, and pubs lie on the route, as you follow the five main river systems of the Peak—Noe, Derwent, Wye, Dove, and Manifold. 52 pages 35 photographs 7 maps
ISBN 0 907496 08 3

PEAK DISTRICT: HIGH LEVEL ROUTE A hard 90 mile, weeks walk, around the Peak District, starting from Matlock. As the title implies the walk keeps to high ground while illustrating the dramatic landscape of the Peak District. The walk was inaugurated and created by John and is used by him for training for his major walks! 60 pages 31 photographs 13 maps
ISBN 0 907496 10 5

PEAK DISTRICT MARATHONS The first reference book to gather together all the major and classical long walks of the Peak District between 25 and 50 miles long. Many are challenge walks with badges and completion cards for those who complete. The longest walk—280 miles —inaugurated by John is around the entire Derbyshire boundary. Each walk has a general map, accommodation list, and details of what guides and maps are needed. 56 pages 20 photographs 20 maps
ISBN 0 907496 13 X

HISTORICAL GUIDES

WINSTER—A VISITOR'S GUIDE A detailed look at a former lead mining community which still retains a Morris dancing team and annual pancake races. A two mile walk brings you to many historical buildings including the 17th century Market House. Illustrated by old photographs. 20 pages 21 photographs 1 map
ISBN 0 907496 21 0

DERBYSHIRE INNS The first book to tell the story behind more than 150 inns in the Peak District and Derbyshire area. With details of legends, murders and historical anecdotes, the book gives added pleasure or impetus to explore the pubs of the region. Profusely illustrated with 65 photographs and a brief history of brewing in Derbyshire. 68 pages 57 photographs 5 maps ISBN 0 907496 11 3

100 HALLS AND CASTLES OF THE PEAK DISTRICT AND DERBYSHIRE A visitor's guide to the principal historical buildings of the region. Many are open to the public and the guide describes the history of the building from the Domesday Book to the present time. The book is illustrated by 120 photographs and makes an excellent souvenir gift of one of England's finest architectural areas. 120 pages 116 photographs 4 maps
ISBN 0 907496 23 7

TOURING THE PEAK DISTRICT AND DERBYSHIRE Twenty circular routes of about 50 miles for the motorist or cyclist. Each route has a set theme, such as the gritstone edges or in the steps of Mary, Queen of Scots. Deatiled maps for each route and fifty photographs make this a useful companion to the Peak District/Derbyshire area. 76 pages 45 photographs 20 maps ISBN 0 907496 22 9

JOHN'S MARATHON WALKS

EMERALD COAST WALK The story of John's walk up the total length of the west coast of Ireland and exploration of more than fifty islands—1,600 miles. 132 pages 32 photographs 12 maps   ISBN 0 907496 02 4

TURN RIGHT AT LAND'S END In 1978 John Merrill became the first person to walk the entire coastline of Britain—6,824 miles in ten months. The book details the route, how he ascended our three major mountains and how he found a wife. Included are more than 200 photographs he took on the walk, which is also a unique guide to our coastline. 246 pages 214 photographs 10 maps
                                                                ISBN 0 907496 24 5

WITH MUSTARD ON MY BACK John has gathered together the stories of his first decade of walking—1970-1980. Here is a collection of unique walks in Britain, from a 2,000 mile walk linking the ten National Parks of England and Wales together to a 450 mile walk from Norwich to Durham. ISBN 0 907496 27 X

TURN RIGHT AT DEATH VALLEY During the summer of 1984, John walked coast to coast across America, a distance of 4,226 miles in 177 days. Few have walked across and none have taken so difficult a route. He crossed all the main mountain ranges, climbed 14,000 foot mountains, crossed deserts in 100 degrees, walked rim to rim of the Grand Canyon in 8 1/2 hours, and crossed the famed Death Valley. The walk is without parallel and the story is the remarkable tale of this unique adventure.   ISBN 0 907496 26 1

Full Moon Inn — Morton — Southwell Walk.

55

WALK RECORD CHART

Date walked

ROCHE ABBEY—7½Miles ....

SOUTH ANSTON AND LINDRICK DALE—5 Miles ....

THORPE SALVIN AND CHESTERFIELD CANAL—3 Miles ....

CARLTON IN LINDRICK—3 Miles ....

WORKSOP AND CHESTERFIELD CANAL—4 Miles ....

WHITWELL AND STEETLEY CHAPEL—5 Miles ....

WELBECK—6, 8 and 14 Miles ....

CRESSWELL CRAGS—3 Miles ....

BARLBOROUGH—4 Miles ....

CLUMBER PARK AND LAKE—6 Miles ....

WALESBY AND BOTHAMSALL—7 Miles ....

SCARCLIFFE AND LANGWITH WOOD—4 Miles ....

BOLSOVER, HARDWICK AND SUTTON SCARSDALE—12 Miles ....

PLEASLEY VALE—4 and 8 Miles ....

WARSOP AND SHERWOOD FOREST—6 Miles ....

EDWINSTOWE AND SHERWOOD FOREST—5 Miles ....

WELLOW—5 Miles ....

RUFFORD ABBEY AND EAKRING—2 and 8 Miles ....

NEWSTEAD ABBEY—7 miles ....

SOUTHWELL AND THE RIVER TRENT—4 and 8 Miles ....

River Trent at Fiskerton Wharf.

56